Thomas Jefferson

A Buddy Book
by
Rebecca Gómez

ABDO
Publishing Company

VISIT US AT

www.abdopub.com

Published by Buddy Books, an imprint of ABDO Publishing Company, 4940 Viking Drive,
Suite 622, Edina, Minnesota 55435. Copyright © 2003 by Abdo Consulting Group, Inc.
International copyrights reserved in all countries. No part of this book may be reproduced in
any form without written permission from the publisher.

Printed in the United States.

Edited by: Christy DeVillier
Contributing Editors: Matt Ray, Michael P. Goecke
Image Research: Deborah Coldiron
Graphic Design: Jane Halbert
Cover Photograph: Library of Congress
Interior Photographs/Illustrations: Getty Images, Library of Congress

Library of Congress Cataloging-in-Publication Data

Gómez, Rebecca.
    Thomas Jefferson / Rebecca Gómez.
       p. cm. — (First biographies. Set III)
    Includes index.
    Summary: A simple biography of the author of the Declaration of Independence,
President of the United States, and founder of the University of Virginia.
    ISBN 1-57765-947-3
    1. Jefferson, Thomas, 1743-1826—Juvenile literature. 2. Presidents—United
States—Biography—Juvenile literature. [1. Jefferson, Thomas, 1743-1826. 2. Presidents.]
    I. Title.

E332.79 .G65 2003
973.4'6'092—dc21
[B]
                             2002074673

Table Of Contents

Who Is Thomas Jefferson?

Thomas Jefferson is an important person in American history. He helped the United States become a country.

Thomas Jefferson wrote the Declaration of Independence. His words "All men are created equal," are famous. Jefferson believed "life, liberty, and the pursuit of happiness" belonged to everyone.

Thomas Jefferson

Growing Up

Thomas Jefferson was born on April 13, 1743. He was born on a farm called Shadwell. Shadwell was in Virginia.

Virginia

Thomas's family moved when he was three years old. They moved to a farm called Tuckahoe. Thomas went to Tuckahoe's schoolhouse. He learned to read and write.

Around age nine, Thomas went to a different school. He learned Latin, Greek, and French. At home, Thomas spent time reading books. He went hunting and fishing with his father. Thomas was only 14 years old when his father died.

Studying Law

At age 17, Thomas Jefferson left home. He moved to Williamsburg, Virginia. Jefferson began studying at the College of William and Mary. In 1762, he began studying law.

This is where Jefferson lived at the College of William and Mary.

In 1769, Jefferson became a member of the House of Burgesses. The House of Burgesses helped the British governor rule Virginia. At that time, Britain ruled the American colonies.

The House of Burgesses inside the Virginia Capitol.

In 1770, Thomas Jefferson met Martha Wayles Skelton. They married in 1772. Thomas and Martha lived in Monticello. Monticello was a house that Jefferson built on a hill in Virginia.

Monticello still stands today in Virginia.

Declaration Of Independence

Over time, American colonists became angry with Britain. They did not like paying high taxes to Britain. In 1775, Americans began fighting the British. This was the beginning of the Revolutionary War.

Benjamin Franklin and others helped Jefferson write the Declaration of Independence.

A famous meeting took place in 1776. It was called the Second Continental Congress. American leaders made plans to break away from Britain. They chose Thomas Jefferson to write America's Declaration of Independence.

On July 4, 1776, American leaders signed the Declaration of Independence.

The Declaration of Independence explains why America wanted its independence. American leaders signed it on July 4, 1776.

After The Revolution

Americans won the Revolutionary War in 1781. The American colonies became the United States of America.

In 1784, Thomas Jefferson moved to Paris, France. The next year, he became the American ambassador to France. Jefferson stayed in France for about five years.

Jefferson (second from right) became the secretary of state in 1790.

In 1790, Thomas Jefferson began working with President George Washington. His title was secretary of state. Later, Jefferson became vice president. He served with President John Adams. John Adams was the second president of the United States.

President Jefferson

In 1801, Thomas Jefferson became the third president of the United States. Under Jefferson's leadership, the United States bought the Louisiana Territory. This was a large area of land west of the Mississippi River.

Third President of the United States

President Jefferson sent men to explore this new land. This famous trip was the Lewis and Clark Expedition. Lewis and Clark discovered the Rocky Mountains for the United States. They found hundreds of plants and animals.

The Louisiana Territory cost the U.S. $15 million.

Louisiana Territory

In 1808, President Jefferson passed a new law. This law made it illegal for Americans to bring over slaves from other countries. This was a big step toward ending slavery. Jefferson hoped America would end slavery one day.

University Of Virginia

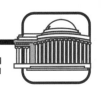

Thomas Jefferson was president for eight years. After being president, he moved back to Monticello. Jefferson spent time with his grandchildren. He farmed wheat and tried to pay his debts.

Thomas Jefferson believed learning was important. He helped to build the University of Virginia. This school opened in 1825.

The University of Virginia stands today in Charlottesville.

An American Hero

On July 4th, 1826, Thomas Jefferson died. Fifty years had passed since American leaders signed the Declaration of Independence.

Inside the Thomas Jefferson Memorial.

WE HOLD THESE TRUTHS TO BE SELF-EVIDENT: THAT ALL MEN ARE CREATED EQUAL, THAT THEY ARE ENDOWED BY THEIR CREATOR WITH CERTAIN INALIENABLE RIGHTS, AMONG THESE ARE LIFE, LIBERTY AND THE PURSUIT OF HAPPINESS, THAT TO SECURE THESE RIGHTS GOVERNMENTS ARE INSTITUTED AMONG MEN. WE... SOLEMNLY PUBLISH AND DECLARE, THAT THESE COLONIES ARE AND OF RIGH OUGHT TO BE FREE AND INDEPENDE STATES...AND FOR THE SUPPORT OF DECLARATION, WITH A FIRM RELI N THE PROTECTION OF D OVIDENCE, WE MUTUALLY PL UR LIVES, OUR FORTUNES AND OUR SACRED HONOUR.

Today, many Americans visit the Thomas Jefferson Memorial. This memorial is in Washington, D.C. It honors Thomas Jefferson's famous words and beliefs.

Thomas Jefferson Memorial at night.

Jefferson's face is the second one from the left on Mount Rushmore.

Another memorial honoring Jefferson is Mount Rushmore. Mount Rushmore is in South Dakota.

Important Dates

1743 Thomas Jefferson is born in Virginia.

1760 Jefferson begins studying at the College of William and Mary.

1768 Jefferson clears land to build Monticello.

1772 Jefferson marries Martha Wayles Skelton.

1776 Jefferson writes the Declaration of Independence.

1779 Jefferson becomes the governor of Virginia.

1781 Americans win the Revolutionary War.

1782 Jefferson's wife, Martha, dies.

1785 Jefferson becomes the American ambassador to France.

1790 Jefferson becomes the United States's secretary of state.

1797 Jefferson becomes vice president of the United States.

1801 Jefferson becomes president of the United States.

1803 The United States buys the Louisiana Territory from France.

1804 Jefferson begins his second term as president.

1825 The University of Virginia opens.

1826 Thomas Jefferson dies on the fourth of July.

Important Words

ambassador the job of speaking for, or representing, one country to other countries.

colony a settlement. A person who lives there is a colonist.

debt money owed to someone.

Declaration of Independence a very important paper in American history. It explains that America is ready to rule itself as an independent country.

memorial something that reminds people of a special person or event.

slave a person who can be bought and sold.

tax money charged by a city or country.

Web Sites

The Presidents of the United States
www.whitehouse.gov/history/presidents/text
Look up facts on Thomas Jefferson and other U.S. presidents.

Monticello—The Home of Thomas Jefferson
www.monticello.org
Learn more about Thomas Jefferson and his home.

Index